The Marble
and Other Ghost Tales of
Tennessee and Virginia

To the Radford Public Library —

Joe Tennis

— Joe Tennis Radford, VA October 29, 2010

Backyardbooks

This work is based on the best references available at the time of research. The author and publisher assume no liabilities arising from use of this book or of its contents. All personal property rights should be respected.

All photographs reproduced in this book are by the author.

ISBN-10: 0-9779443-4-4
ISBN-13: 978-0-9779443-4-7
Copyright © 2007 by Joe Tennis
Printed in the United States of America
All Rights Reserved

3 4 5 6 7 8 9 0

For my wife, Mary

Acknowledgments

For help in completing this book, foremost thanks to Daniel Lewis, Sherry Lewis, Karin O'Brien Archer Blevins, and Bill May, Jr.

Additional thanks to family members: Maggie Caudill; James and Melissa Caudill; Steve and Stephanie Talbert; Richard and Jeanette Tennis; Rob Tennis; Josephine Boswell; Angie Broyles Wolfe; my son, John Patrick; and my daughter, Abigail.

Several people also shared stories or simply provided encouragement with this project, including Tim Cable, Rex McCarty, Rita Walters, Bobbi Potter, Garnett Gilliam, Charlie Engle, Amy Clark, Jane Meade Dean, "Papa" Joe Smiddy, Elizabeth Wills, Bob and Suzy Harrison, Ann and Allen Gregory, Patsy Phillips, Jim Baldwin, Louise Leslie, Dirk Moore, Mary Blevins, Claude Lewis, John Sauers, Skip Blackburn, Max Hermann, Bill McKee, Pete Sheffey, Donnamarie Emmert, Richard Rose, Courtney Bledsoe, Shelby Edwards, Darlene Cole, David McGee, Melvin Boyd, Jan Patrick, Bill Milhorn, Roger Hartley, Judy and Robert Hotchkiss, Chad Bogart, Sue Carney, Marcy Hawley, Claudia Moody, Jimmy Neil Smith, Linda Poland, Sue Henley, Julia Beach, Linda Black, and Dixie Blackman.

I also want to thank V. N. "Bud" Phillips, a longtime friend, for sharing his stories and encouraging me to develop a version of "Rooster Ghosts." His own version of this story can be found in his book *Pioneers in Paradise*.

Contents

Introduction

When parents want to keep their children inside at night, they sometimes make up a scary story. Or they might repeat a tale they heard from their own childhood. Either reason might be why a big boulder east of Damascus, Virginia, came to be called "The Booger Rock." Here, legend says, you must not venture out after dark, or a "Booger" will get you.

Is that true? Who knows?

But the Booger Rock is a place that has certainly made more than one child scared. And it represents much of what this book is about—stories that have been told and how people have reacted to them.

The Marble and Other Ghost Tales of Tennessee and Virginia collects twenty-two stories from places across the Mountain Empire, including Greeneville, Abingdon, Kingsport, Bristol, Big Stone Gap, and Johnson City. Each is based on a blend of folk legends, longtime traditions, historical research, and firsthand accounts.

The Lost Orphan Girls

No one really knows how Wadlow Gap got its name. But there's a story that says this narrow passage from Kingsport, Tennessee, into Scott County, Virginia, used to be called "Waterloo," and that name has slowly evolved into "Wadlow."

Likewise, no one really knows much about a particular black couple who lived at Wadlow Gap in 1865. But a story that has been passed down through the generations says these former slaves were poor, defenseless, and vulnerable to plundering.

Shortly after the end of the Civil War, the couple met their fate at the hands of ragtag troops. Returning home from battlefields tired, hungry, and desperate, the soldiers slaughtered the couple, burned their cabin, and stole whatever they did not destroy.

The couple's young daughters, however, ran into the woods. And now the lost orphan girls, eight and ten years old, had to fend for themselves. They lived in their barn, because nobody wanted to take them in since they were children of former slaves.

One local farmer, a white man, did try to help by

The Homeplace Mountain Farm and Museum lies at Wadlow Gap, Virginia.

bringing food to the girls. But during the winter, while the farmer was gone for several days, the temperature fell into the teens and snow began to fall. When the man returned, he found one of the girls frozen to death, so he buried her on a rocky hill.

The farmer continued to look after the other girl. But after another trip, he returned to find she had fallen asleep forever—frozen—atop the grave of her sister.

Over the next century, the graves of both girls would be nearly lost on a hill among the ivy-covered rocks of Wadlow Gap. At this place, in a field, the Homeplace Mountain Farm and Museum was built with several old cabins to show what life was like at Wadlow Gap around the time of the Civil War.

Schoolchildren come to the Homeplace on field trips. And, naturally, they laugh in the summertime sun.

But a man working at the Homeplace once heard mysterious giggling—the laughter of what sounds like two girls playing in the field—when no one else was around. Other times, as the cold of winter brings snow, legend says that you can hear the ghostly voices of those lost orphan girls.

And you can hear them cry.

Woman in the Window

Elizabeth Morris came from Keokee, Virginia, in the 1890s to live at what is now the June Tolliver House at Big Stone Gap. She stayed only three months, but that was long enough for writer John Fox, Jr. to partially base the character of June Tolliver on the young schoolgirl in his 1908 novel *Trail of the Lonesome Pine*. It was also just enough time to make some people believe Elizabeth might now be haunting the handsome house.

Painted in red and gold, the June Tolliver House serves as headquarters and a gift shop for summer productions of an outdoor drama based on Fox's novel. The Queen Anne-style home, built around 1890, was a boardinghouse when Elizabeth lived in it.

In 1964, the same year the outdoor drama began, Nick Botts visited Big Stone Gap with his sister, Becky Arnott. The pair passed by the June Tolliver House—at the time, locked and empty—and Nick snapped a photo. Later, when he had the picture developed, he noticed the figure of a woman standing behind one of the second-floor windows. The woman

The June Tolliver House at Big Stone Gap, Virginia

looked ghostly and appeared to be holding something in her hands—possibly a candle, maybe a baby. Either way, the image of that woman in the window has never been explained.

Neither has the vision of what longtime June Tolliver House worker Bobbi Potter once saw: the wispy shadow of a woman passing by a window on the backside of the house. But, Potter said, this apparition didn't walk by. It floated by.

Mysterious Martha

The Bible says all things will return to dust. But for one little girl in Wise, Virginia, the vision of seeing dust turn into things that talked would prove so haunting that she would be too frightened to sleep alone.

It happened on the campus of the University of Virginia's College at Wise. Formerly known as "Clinch Valley College," this school was built on the site of the old Wise County Poor Farm, a place where unfortunate and destitute people lived in the early 20th century.

Much of the college landscape has changed over the years. And, in some cases, so have the names of buildings. The college's Bowers-Sturgill Hall was once called Martha Randolph Hall, taking its name from a daughter of President Thomas Jefferson, founder of the original University of Virginia at Charlottesville. Even earlier, this stone building was known as a home for "wayward women." And here, legend says, one young pregnant woman hung herself from a set of pipes inside the building until she died.

Bowers-Sturgill Hall
was once known as Martha Randolph Hall.

Today, some believe, the ghost of that young woman has appeared inside the hall and continues to reappear, especially to young children.

During the 1980s, strange hauntings happened to the family of the college's housing director at an apartment inside the hall. One time, the director heard the call of his name—"Charlie!"—when no one else was around. Sometimes, too, Charlie would hang his keys on a hook, only to find them turn up in an odd place, like under the kitchen sink.

After a while, Charlie's family gave a name to their ghost—"Martha"—since they lived in what was then Martha Randolph Hall. But they grew worried as the ghost of mysterious Martha seemed to appear to Charlie's three-year-old daughter. Sometimes the daughter would play in her room alone but tell her parents she had been talking to "the girl."

"The girl?" her parents would ask.

"The girl who hangs off the pipe," Charlie's daughter would say.

And, yet, Charlie's daughter may not have been the only child haunted by Martha.

About thirty years earlier, in the mid-1950s, a biology teacher lived in this building with his family, including a four-year-old daughter. Often she would tell her parents that the dust in the corners of her room would turn into people who could talk to her.

The little girl's mother thought such a story

sounded like rubbish. "There is no dust in here," she would say. "This house is clean!"

But the young girl insisted that, just as she fell asleep, the dust would materialize into individuals who could speak. She could not remember who these creatures were or what they said. But they frightened her.

And, for years afterward, she refused to sleep alone.

The Clinch River Cliff

Every once in a while, you'll see somebody lounging by the Clinch River in St. Paul, Virginia. They might be camping or just hanging out with friends. But if they're staring at a high cliff above the water, they may just be on the lookout for the mysterious lady in white.

This ghostly woman is said to jump from the cliff on the Russell County side of town. And, yet, she never makes a splash. As legend tells it, the lady in white disappears before ever hitting the water.

Some people believe this woman may be connected to the town's tragic beginnings.

In the 1880s, a group of businessmen proposed big dreams for St. Paul, with plans to construct a set of twin cities, similar to those in Minnesota, on the banks of the Clinch River. The cliff above the Clinch, in Russell County, was dubbed "Minneapolis," while the other side, in Wise County, was called "St. Paul."

Tragedy struck about 1890, when some promoters for a railroad line through the town were killed.

Nearly all development came to a halt. The town of Minneapolis, subsequently, just never came to be.

Even so, people now believe that the ghostly lady in white remembers this tragedy. They say she jumps toward the river to mourn the loss of her true love—one of the railroad's early promoters, who died in the untimely accident.

The Principal Who Never Left School

At night, sometimes, A. P. Baldwin would leave his house and go next door to Honaker High School. There, it is said, he would pace the hallways and smoke cigarettes.

Today, some believe, Baldwin still does so—as a ghost—inside the A. P. Baldwin Gymnasium in Honaker, Virginia. At night, people say, they can see mysterious red dots—the fiery glow at the end of Baldwin's cigarettes—inside the school gym.

Born in 1912, Baldwin began teaching in the 1930s. By the middle of World War II, he had moved to the principal's chair at Honaker High School, where he remained for thirty-three years. Students and teachers remember him as a tall man with broad shoulders and a long, narrow face. He liked a joke as much as he liked to smoke.

Soon after Baldwin died in 1981, Honaker's ghost stories began. People reported seeing ghostly cigarette tips above the bleachers in the gymnasium. For a while, it even became in vogue for students to sneak into the school at night and hold seances on the gym floor.

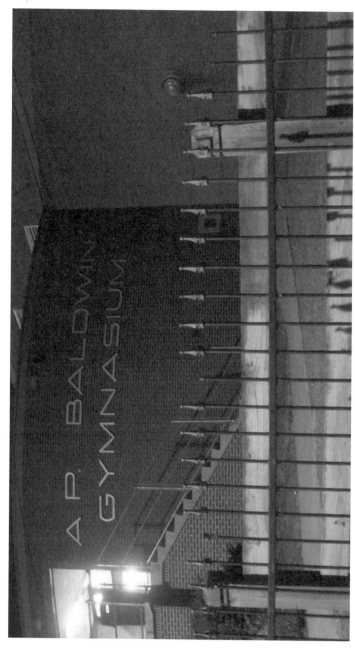

At night, it's said, you can see the ghost of A. P. Baldwin smoking cigarettes at Honaker High School.

Then came that legendary evening in the early 1990s. Two teachers and a few students went into the gym after baseball practice just after seven-thirty. The lights were on but all of a sudden began to flicker, going almost completely out—except for one right above the high-jump mat. That one light, a teacher said, "turned blood red."

Next came sightings of something in the balcony. What showed up, according to the teachers, appeared to be a huge silhouette wearing a cape—or what might have been a trench coat covering a man with broad shoulders.

"He was real tall," one teacher remembered, "and we could see coming out of his mouth the glow of a cigarette. You could see the little red glow." The teacher said the silhouette then "went from one end of the batting cage all the way to the other, almost in an instant."

Two students screamed and ran out of the gym. Both teachers, meanwhile, ran to the balcony to investigate. One said he found ashes on the floor where the smoking apparition had stood.

To this day, many believe, the ghost keeps smoking. At least, no one can explain why, at night, people see what looks like the red tips of lit cigarettes in the gymnasium balcony—what some say is a sign of the principal who never left school.

Haunts of the French House

From the mid 1980s until 2006, guests stayed overnight at the J. Stewart French House on the campus of Emory & Henry College. But many swore they would never stay again, reporting ghostly happenings inside the historic landmark.

Built in 1852 as a faculty residence, the house dates to the earliest decades of the Methodist college, founded in 1836 a few miles north of Abingdon, Virginia. The French House took its name from the college's colorful eleventh president, who, in the 1920s, was known to scandalize the college community simply because he smoked cigars and played golf. The brick landmark served as a home for college presidents from the 1890s until 1964.

One time, an overnight guest in the French House reported hearing a piano play. Another talked about a levitating bed. Someone else claimed to see a small child walk into a room. At night, some say, you can feel a cold breeze inside the house, followed by the sound of a slamming door.

The most convincing accounts of unexplained

J. Stewart French House on the campus of Emory & Henry College

forces, however, come from two different people on separate occasions. They said that while lying in bed they felt someone tap them on their shoulder in the middle of the night. And then? Turning over, neither found anyone else in the room.

The Creekfield Woman

Some say she had black hair. Others say it was blonde. Either way, at some point in the early 1900s, farmers began spotting "The Creekfield Woman" in Green Cove, not far from where Virginia meets both Tennessee and North Carolina.

A largely isolated spot, Green Cove, Virginia, takes its name from a green forest of pine trees. At the dawn of the 20th century, those trees were cut and shipped as timber on the Virginia-Carolina Railroad, nicknamed "The Virginia Creeper." Here, legend says, the Creekfield Woman could sometimes be seen on a ridgetop near Chestnut Mountain or in cleared fields, close to the gurgling waters of Green Cove Creek.

Stories contend that the Creekfield Woman had lost a child or that her child was snatched from her. Some even believed that if you followed this beautiful woman, she would lead you to a buried treasure.

Sightings occurred from the early 1900s to the early 1950s. Then, for decades, no one seemed to mention her.

Some say "The Creekfield Woman" can be seen near Green Cove Creek.

Now, possibly, the Creekfield Woman has returned. What used to be the railroad running through Green Cove is now the Virginia Creeper Trail. And local legend says the trail's consistent activity has since made the Creekfield Woman reappear.

After Midnight

After midnight, lights go out at The Tavern in Abingdon, Virginia, and the restaurant staff goes home. That's a rule. From midnight until the next morning at nine o'clock, according to restaurant owner Max Hermann, the town's oldest structure is given back to the spirits.

What spirits? Well, there may be a different kind of spirits than what's served at the bar. People have reported doors opening and no one coming through, glasses falling off shelves, and footsteps in the attic—all after midnight.

Built in 1779 as a tavern and overnight inn for stagecoach travelers, the handsome landmark looks like it would be naturally at home on the streets of Williamsburg. Still standing on its original site at 222 East Main Street, the building has also housed a bank, a bakery, a barbershop, a private residence, a general store, a cabinet shop, an antique shop, and a post office.

During the Civil War, the third-floor attic of The Tavern served as a field hospital for wounded soldiers.

The Tavern on Abingdon's Main Street

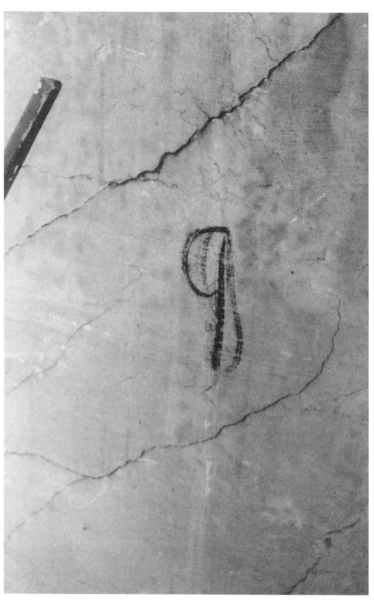

Numbers to designate patients' beds were etched with charcoal on the plaster walls of The Tavern's third-floor attic.

Numbers designating patients' beds were etched in charcoal on the attic's plaster walls.

Those numbers remain today. And they can be frightening.

In the late 1970s, Hermann says, a repairman installed a heating and air-conditioning system in The Tavern and learned the location of all of the building's wires. The repairman told The Tavern's owners to contact him if he was ever needed again. But not at night, he stressed, and never after midnight.

One time when the lights were out, the repairman said, those numbers on the wall lit up—going from a charcoal black to an eerie blood red. Hurriedly, the repairman grabbed his tools and fled, swearing to never again return to The Tavern after dark.

Cat in the Bed

Ghost stories at the Martha Washington Inn in Abingdon, Virginia, often date to the days of the Civil War—a time when Confederates guarded the village as Union troops marched through town. Leftover tales from that era include sightings of a riderless horse on the hotel's south lawn. Sometimes, at night, legend says, this ghostly animal can be seen galloping—forever looking in vain for its master, a soldier killed during a skirmish near the end of 1864.

From that tragic time in the 1860s until the Great Depression in the 1930s, the stately hotel on Main Street housed the Martha Washington College. And today, many believe, the spirits of some college students linger within the building's walls.

In luxurious quarters known as the Napoleon Room, hotel tour guide Pete Sheffey says, a guest in her mid eighties tried to take an afternoon nap but could not get to sleep after hearing a strange noise. And then she saw what looked like a young college student floating in the corner—with black hair, a hat, and an apron-type dress. The startled old woman

Martha Washington Inn of Abingdon, Virginia

called for her daughter, yelling, "Mary! Someone's in the room!"

The daughter walked in and asked what was the matter. But the ghostly girl had vanished.

Who was she? Who knows?

Inside a different guest room, Sheffey says, the spirit of a cat that once slept with the college students has now curled into a fuzzy ghost.

He said a young girl sleeping in the room with her parents awoke in the middle of the night, crying, "Mommy, there's a cat in the bed. Mommy! Look at the cat, Mommy!"

The young girl's parents jumped up, Sheffey said, and the ghostly cat disappeared. Immediately, a night auditor and housekeeper came to inspect the room. The ghostly cat was never located, Sheffey added, but cat hair was found on the bed.

Spirit of the Stage

Robert Porterfield's death in 1971 may not have truly meant curtains for the founder of the Barter Theatre. For decades, people say, the beloved Porterfield has been seen as the spirit of the stage in Abingdon, Virginia.

Porterfield, an actor in New York in the 1920s, came home to Virginia as the Great Depression made jobs on stages scarce. Showing up in Abingdon, he developed the idea for a "barter" theatre—a place where people could pay admission to see plays, even if they had no money.

His idea was simple. The word *barter* means to trade. And that's exactly what people did: trade eggs, barley, chickens, or tobacco to get into Porterfield's place. The idea worked so well that, by the end of the first season in 1933, his troupe of twenty-two once-starving actors boasted a collective weight gain of more than 300 pounds!

Porterfield continued to guide the Barter Theatre until he died at age sixty-five. Soon after, the first so-called "Porterfield sightings" began. Actors and stage-

Barter Theatre in Abingdon, Virginia

hands reported seeing the ghost of a familiar-looking, yet unknown older man inside the theatre, usually wearing a white dinner jacket or gray sweater. Some surmised this to be Porterfield, known affectionately as "Mr. P."

Over the years, Barter Theatre officials have not dismissed the Porterfield sightings. Actually, to the contrary, they have even produced a video highlighting the history of the theatre, including scenes of actors demonstrating how the ghost of "Mr. P" might be seen standing next to a wall or sitting in the audience, watching the stage that he loved so well.

Return of the Roosters

The line where Bristol, Virginia, meets Bristol, Tennessee, can be confusing, especially at East Hill Cemetery. According to local lore, some folks have their heads buried in Virginia and their feet in Tennessee, because the state line has changed slightly over the course of a century and a half.

Prior to the establishment of the cemetery in 1857, the area was known as Rooster Hill, a name that stems from rounds of popular cockfights held on the property. Here, roosters attacked each other, leaving the ground soaked with blood and scattered with carcasses.

Rough men in Bristol attended these fights and placed bets on which rooster would survive the longest. One promoter of such struggles was Webb Sykes, an ex-convict and one of Bristol's earliest settlers.

Not everyone liked Sykes. Some claimed he was a cheat in business deals. He died in 1874, nearly broke, and had few, if any, friends.

His funeral was held at the site of his former cockfights at what was then called Round Hill Cemetery, later renamed East Hill. But during the proceedings,

East Hill Cemetery in Bristol

a loud clucking and clatter suddenly arose. Ghostly roosters could be heard crowing, as men with ropes tried to lower the coffin into the ground.

No actual roosters were seen, remembered "Old Daddy" Thomas, who attended the funeral. But all at once, it seemed the ghosts of roosters had arrived, like a feathered army wanting revenge against Sykes for making them fight and kill each other.

In a frenzy, the men holding ropes on Sykes's coffin suddenly let go, and the casket dropped into the ground. Thomas and others became so scared that they ran away.

As for the roosters, they just kept on crowing, all the way to dark.

Bristol

Phantom Train

Students and teachers at Bristol Tennessee High School report hearing the ghostly sounds of a phantom train as it moves from the gymnasium through the hallways. Although the train can be heard, it is never seen.

What might explain the sound stems from a legend that predates the campus.

Long before Tennessee High School was built in 1939, trees covered the school grounds. In this area, called "The Flatwoods," a civil engineer in the late 1800s proposed building a railroad line. Unfortunately, he could not muster support for his plan. And, as legend goes, the man threatened to kill himself if he did not get his way.

Sadly, that's what he did. The man supposedly shot himself under a massive beech tree near where the high school now stands.

A railroad line does come through Bristol, but not here. More than a century later, however, many believe this engineer made a train come down his intended path, after all.

Tennessee High School at Bristol

Right down the hallway of the high school, people say they hear the mysterious *chug-chug-chug* of a train, following down the railroad tracks that were never built.

Ghostly George

Employees at the *Sullivan County News* once believed a ghost inhabited the newspaper's simple block building. People working downstairs said they could hear noises coming from upstairs, as if a door was opening and ghostly footsteps traced the floor. Upon investigation, however, the employees would see nothing.

But there must have been something—at least once. As the story goes, somebody actually shot at a ghost in this building along State Highway 126 in Blountville, Tennessee. Details remain sketchy, but one newspaper employee recalled helping others dig a bullet out of a wall.

The newspaper staff reported their resident ghost often hid things, or moved things, such as X-acto knives or a pair of pliers. Some even said they saw the ghost of "George," wearing a gray suit.

Still, how this ghost came to be called "George" has nothing to do with any haunting; rather, it stems from a joke. One day, an employee named George startled another, and everyone else laughed. Later, some decided, "George" also sounded like a good name for the newspaper's ghost.

The now-defunct newspaper once shared its building with an insurance office. Part of the same building, legend says, also at one time housed a pool hall, where a fight broke out and someone was killed. People subsequently surmised that whoever lost his life came back as "Ghostly George."

The Marble

Sometimes you can hear voices coming out of various chambers of the Appalachian Caverns in the center of Sullivan County, Tennessee, even though no one else is around. Could these voices be ghosts? Well, probably not. Such sounds are likely the echoes of people carrying on conversations inside homes built above the cavern's countless crevices.

Decades ago, before Appalachian Caverns opened to the public for tours, this attraction near Blountville was called the "Linville Cave," named for a local Linville family. Still standing today near the cavern entrance is what's known as the Linville Cabin. The structure likely was built around 1777, as evidenced by that number etched into a brick on the side of the fireplace.

But something more than the cabin may be leftover from the 1770s—a spirit. Some believe the Linville Cabin is haunted, based on sightings that began in 2005, six years after the cabin's last human resident moved out.

One night, according to a volunteer at the

Linville Cabin, near Appalachian Caverns

Appalachian Caverns, the log cabin's chandelier swayed without a breeze and a jack-o'-lantern fell off the porch and rolled uphill. The volunteer also recalled that one day while the cabin was closed and empty, people saw a candle and a shadowy image pass by a window.

Another time, a man working inside the cabin heard a marble roll across the floor. He turned and saw a little boy wearing clothes from the Colonial-era. The ghostly boy held a finger to his lips and looked at the man, as if to say, "Shh! Be quiet!"

Mysteriously, the next day, a different man discovered a white clay marble—the kind used as toys in the 1770s, about the time the cabin was built.

Spookiness at Prospect Hill

Something—or some spirit—favoring bourbon and peanut butter cookies is said to create spookiness at Prospect Hill, a bed-and-breakfast in Mountain City, Tennessee.

The inn occupies one of the town's most lavish landmarks, the Wagner-Rambo House. The "Wagner" name comes from Maj. Joseph Wagner, a Mountain City man who served in the Union Army during the Civil War and built the house in 1889. The "Rambo" comes from a local family who purchased the house in 1910.

By 1999, Judy and Robert Hotchkiss had acquired Prospect Hill with plans to open a bed-and-breakfast. About this time, while in the course of extensive renovations, Judy reported hearing loud, unexplained footsteps inside the house, like somebody walking across the floor in heavy shoes.

After the inn opened, an overnight guest came to Prospect Hill's breakfast table one morning expecting a certain treat. In the middle of the night, the young man said, he could distinctly smell the aroma

Prospect Hill Bed-and-Breakfast at Mountain City

of peanut butter cookies baking in the kitchen. But he was mistaken—there were no such cookies in the house!

Another time, a man stepped out of a bathtub in a guest room and said he could smell bourbon. But, like the cookies, there was nothing of that sort at Prospect Hill.

Perhaps the strangest story comes from a man who stayed overnight but could not get to sleep. And why? Because, he said, the ghost of a man in old-fashioned clothes sat in a chair and stared at him the entire night.

Ghost of the Carter Mansion

John Carter came to Northeast Tennessee prior to the American Revolution, settling what became Carter's Valley between Rogersville and Kingsport. He also set stakes along the Watauga River.

Around 1780, Carter began construction of what is now the oldest frame house in Tennessee. Overlooking the Watauga River, the Carter Mansion stands among the ancient oaks of Elizabethton and is shown to visitors as an affiliate of the nearby Sycamore Shoals State Historic Park.

The white two-story house features hand-hewn timbers, elegant crown molding, glass panes, and chair rails. It would have been considered quite a mansion in its early days, when mostly shacks and log cabins stood along the sparsely settled Watauga River region, then a part of North Carolina.

Sadly, Carter did not live long enough to enjoy the home.

When Carter died in 1781, his son, Landon, and Landon's wife, Elizabeth, inherited the mansion. Landon Carter would be remembered in the name of

Carter Mansion at Elizabethton, Tennessee

"Carter County," while Elizabeth's name was forever enshrined as "Elizabethton."

Upstairs, the Carter couple's seven children are thought to have stayed in the room that has no fireplace. Looking at the Carter Mansion from Broad Street Extension, that room would be behind the upper-right corner window.

Look closely in that window. Sometimes, a tour guide says, you can see the figure of a girl—possibly the ghost of one of Landon and Elizabeth's daughters.

Scares of the Sherrod Library

For years, students at East Tennessee State University in Johnson City have told of the scares of the Sherrod Library. But it's not that the students fear an overwhelming homework assignment might force them into the library for what seems like forever. Instead, they believe the ghost of a librarian hovers inside the brick building named for Charles C. Sherrod, the university's second president.

Some think the matronly librarian keeps an eye on the archives at this landmark. Common stories say you may feel like you're being watched while browsing bookshelves.

Another legend says a shadowy figure lurks in the library. And something has even been seen floating down a staircase.

Yet the old library is only one place at ETSU that people claim is haunted. Around the campus, stories say unexplainable footsteps can be heard in Mathes Music Hall. A screaming ghost could once be heard in Cooper Hall, a building that no longer stands.

Charles C. Sherrod Library on the campus of
East Tennessee State University

The spirit of the university's first president, Sidney Gilbreath, is also thought to remain on campus. Some believe that his ghost is what mysteriously closes windows inside Gilbreath Hall, a building named in his honor.

Devil's Looking Glass

All across the Appalachians, places are named for the devil—from a boulder called the Devil's Head at Chimney Rock, North Carolina, to a summit known as the Devil's Nose near Rogersville, Tennessee. In Virginia, you'll find a small cliff named the Devil's Armchair near Christiansburg and a gap called the Devil's Racepath near Duffield.

Where does the devil get clean? Why, in the Devil's Bathtub, of course! That's a hole in a creek that actually looks like a bathtub, just north of Fort Blackmore, Virginia.

The Devil's Looking Glass, part of which lies in the Cherokee National Forest, can be seen from several points around Erwin, Tennessee. The best place to view the cliff is from the deck of the River's Edge Restaurant in Unicoi County.

Often, places were named for the devil because they were located in rough terrain or they attracted crass characters. Many of these places look strange, or simply spooky.

The Devil's Looking Glass is no exception, with

Some say you can see the faces of devils in the crevices of the
Devil's Looking Glass, rising above the Nolichucky River,
in Unicoi County, Tennessee.

its rocky cliff that towers 300 feet above the rampaging rapids of the Nolichucky River. And, if you look hard enough, people say, you can see the faces of devils in the crevices of the sheer rock wall.

One tale of how the place came to be called the Devil's Looking Glass is owed to an English translation of the words *la Espejo de el Diablo*—the name given to the formation by early Spanish explorers.

Other stories say Native Americans have jumped from the cliff—and their ghosts remain.

Giggling Ghosts

Men can hear them, but women can't. These "giggling ghosts" reside at the Rees-Hawley House, a bed-and-breakfast in Jonesborough, Tennessee.

Advertisements say this house is "The Oldest Building In Tennessee's Oldest Town." No one really knows how many uses the rambling landmark has seen over the course of more than two centuries. Originally the home of James Rees, it was built in 1793 on Lot No. 1 in Jonesborough.

Innkeeper Marcy Hawley named one of her corner guest rooms for Gen. Francis Preston, a former owner. In the Preston Room, Hawley said, is where the giggling goes on.

One man stayed in an adjacent guest room and later asked who was in the Preston Room making so much noise. But as for women, Hawley said, they simply do not notice—or cannot hear—the Preston Room's alleged combination of girlish giggles and faint chatter.

Rees-Hawley House, a bed-and-breakfast at Jonesborough, Tennessee

Apparition of Andy

You can plainly see him on your twenty-dollar bills with his wild shock of hair. Longstanding legend says you can see his ghost walking down Main Street in Jonesborough, Tennessee.

Meet President Andrew Jackson—or Andy, as he was known as a young man when he rode a racehorse into Jonesborough in 1788. Carrying a couple of pistols, Andy must have looked tough. The future president was a regular character in the town for fifteen years, off and on, first as a lawyer, then as a judge.

But only weeks after his initial arrival, twenty-one-year-old Andy found himself challenging Waightstill Avery, an attorney more than twice his age, to a duel. Avery had ridiculed the younger man for making many references to Matthew Bacon's *Abridgement of the Law* during a court trial. The next day, Andy slipped Avery a note stating that his "feelings and character are injured" and he wanted "to seek a speedy redress."

The two lawyers met that afternoon on a hillside, but their duel ended with both men firing shots into the air. No one was hurt.

Christopher Taylor House in Jonesborough, Tennessee

But could Jackson's spirit today still be pining for his younger days in Jonesborough? Some say his presence hovers near the Christopher Taylor House, next door to the Chester Inn. Jackson lived at the Christopher Taylor House in 1788 when it stood about a mile west of town. Built in the late 1770s, the log house was moved in 1974 to Jonesborough's Main Street.

The Chester Inn, constructed in 1797, was named for its builder, Dr. William P. Chester of Lancaster, Pennsylvania. When Jackson was President of the United States, he held a reception for his friends on the Chester Inn's porch during the summer of 1832.

Maybe that wasn't his last visit.

In 2002, two middle-aged couples allegedly saw an apparition of Andy near the Eureka Hotel, which also stands on Jonesborough's Main Street. One of the women in the foursome said she had heard about Jackson-in-Jonesborough sightings, but she had no basis to believe—until that night in July.

"There was this gentleman dressed in a long topcoat, dressed down to his boots, dressed solidly black," the woman recalled. "And this figure walked down to the edge of the sidewalk and walked to the side of the Eureka Hotel."

At one point, the man turned his head, the woman said, but no one could catch a glimpse of his face.

And then?

"He totally disappeared into the parking lot," she said. "And he hadn't been in the parking lot more than a few seconds. There was nothing in that parking lot. No cars—no anything."

The couples later discovered nothing was happening that night at the Jonesborough Repertory Theater or at the Eureka Hotel—at least, there was nothing to explain the odd-dressed man they saw.

Green Room Grace

Places are painted green all over Greeneville, Tennessee. Pay no mind, though, because Greeneville was actually named for Maj. Gen. Nathanael Greene, a Revolutionary War hero. People in Greeneville, regardless, talk about "Keeping the Green in Greene," like green is the city's color scheme.

Of course, green would be all you could call the "Green Room" at the General Morgan Inn. This handsome dining hall boasts green wallpaper, green drapes, green carpet—even green fabric on its wooden chairs. It is one of a handful of the hotel's dining rooms and the only one believed to be haunted by a spoon-snatching waitress.

The General Morgan Inn first opened as the Grand Central Hotel on Greeneville's Main Street in 1890. Then, for years, it was called the Hotel Brumley. Scores of regulars poured into the Brumley Coffee Shop, especially on Sundays. But after 1981, the hotel and its restaurant stood still—and deteriorated—while awaiting a much-celebrated renovation.

Soon after the General Morgan Inn opened in

The General Morgan Inn in Greeneville, Tennessee

1996, staff members surmised not only guests but ghosts wandered around the century-old structure. For proof, front-desk employees point to the curtains in the far-left corner window of the hotel lobby, just above the ballroom doors. Those curtains, they say, sometimes move.

Is that strange? Well, yes, since there's nothing behind that decorative window but a brick wall!

In the hotel restaurant, a hostess said she once saw a shadowy figure pass between dining rooms. Also, the staff says, silverware often turns up missing in the Green Room—but not a knife and never a fork; it's always a snatched spoon. Staff members blame such losses on "Green Room Grace," said to be the spirit of a waitress who likes to reset tables.

Frights of the Sensabaugh Tunnel

Kingsport's creepy Sensabaugh Tunnel would be scary even if it had no ghost story. Its concrete walls, covered with unsightly graffiti, look cracked, and the passage itself is so narrow that vehicles cannot pass each other.

What's more, consider the games some people play, stopping their cars in the middle of the 100-foot-long tunnel. Whether by day or by night, they test so-called spirits, just to see if something might make a noise.

Obviously, you'll hear the rippling waters of the Sensabaugh Branch rush through this 1920s-era tunnel in Hawkins County, Tennessee. But ghost hunters come here listening for much more, despite the debates on what might happen—or even if anything ever did.

Stories change with nearly every account of the Sensabaugh Tunnel. Countless Internet sites pay tribute to the gloomy-looking place with blogs, videos, firsthand observations, and even some spooky stuff that seems straight out of fiction.

The eerie Sensabaugh Tunnel at Kingsport, Tennessee, has attracted a series of legends.

Some say a hobo killed a baby inside the tunnel. Others tell stories of a murderer named Sensabaugh. Some say an entire family was killed. Another version says a pregnant girl died inside. And then some say that all this stuff about the Sensabaugh Tunnel is just a myth—or, even, that all spooks stem from a long-running series of practical jokes!

One school of thought says the automobile passage called Sensabaugh Tunnel is not technically the "right" tunnel. What's actually haunted, the purists say, is a nearby railroad passage—the "real" Sensabaugh Tunnel.

But, of course, there will always be believers—the ones who insist you can hear phantom footsteps. They'll say a car won't start again if it stops inside the tunnel. And then? They'll say you can hear the haunting cries of a baby.

Is that true? The believers claim it is!

Select Bibliography

Aird, Brandon and Diane Silver, ed. *Time It Was: Snapshots of Emory & Henry College.* Emory, Va.: self-published, 2004.

Barefoot, Daniel J. *Haunted Halls of Ivy.* Winston-Salem, N.C.: John F. Blair, Publisher, 2004.

Dawidziak, Mark. *The Barter Theatre Story: Love Made Visible.* Boone, N.C.: Appalachian Consortium Press, 1982.

Phillips, V. N. (Bud). *Pioneers In Paradise.* Johnson City, Tenn.: The Overmountain Press, 2002.

Price, Charles Edwin. *Haunted Jonesborough.* Johnson City, Tenn.: The Overmountain Press, 1993.

Price, Charles Edwin. *More Haunted Tennessee.* Johnson City, Tenn.: The Overmountain Press, 1999.

Saint Paul Tomorrow. "Strategic Plan for the Town of

St. Paul, Virginia." St. Paul, Va.: self-published, 2005.

Smith, Jimmy Neil. "Andy's Ghost Roams Jonesborough Streets." *The Historical News,* June 2005.

Smith, Jimmy Neil. *Heritage in Buckskin.* Johnson City, Tenn.: Don and Mignon Printing, 1971.

Smith, Rain. "Spirits Said to Linger Throughout Historic Abingdon." *Washington County News.* 30 October 2002.

"Spirited Specters Stay on at Historic Hotels." Norfolk, Va.: *The Flagship.* 26 September 2006.

Tennis, Joe. "Haunted Hallways: Longtime Principal Is Said to Haunt Honaker High School." *Bristol Herald Courier.* 30 October 2005.

Tennis, Joe. "Haunted Hallways: Mystery of the Swinging Light Haunts Emory & Henry College." *Bristol Herald Courier.* 27 October 2005.

"There's Real 'Magic' in These Mountains." *Bristol Herald Courier.* 25 October 1987.

Also by Joe Tennis

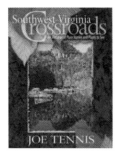

Southwest Virginia Crossroads, published by The Overmountain Press, proves the state does not stop at Roanoke! From Abingdon to Blacksburg, this illustrated history and guide tells how more than 750 places took their names, and points the way to 50 waterfalls and 26 lakes. Explore legends, landmarks, mountain music venues, natural wonders, trails, parks, fishing holes, and roadside curiosities in this scenic 17-county region.

ISBN: 1-57072-256-0 • $29.95

"It's a mesmerizing, detailed, brilliantly researched account of our region which will make the public proud of where they came from."
—C. Robert Weisfeld
Abingdon Virginian

"A crackerjack guidebook. . . . A jewel box of wayfaring treasure."
—Bill Ruehlmann
The Virginian-Pilot

"Fascinating and well-illustrated."
—George Thwaites
Kingsport Times-News

"Possibly the most comprehensive body of work on the rural mountainous western part of the state."
—Lynn Davis
The Roanoke Times

"The kind of book you want to own."
—Valley Haggard
Style Weekly

Also by Joe Tennis

Fall 2007 release from
The Overmountain Press

Take a trip across Virginia—from Cape Henry to Cumberland Gap. *Beach to Bluegrass* serves tales of triumph and tragedy, sandwiched between the "Gateway to the New World" and the "Gateway to the West." The 58-chapter story lies largely along Virginia's longest road—US-58—an east-to-west highway that spans more than 500 miles and passes through every type of town and terrain imaginable in the Old Dominion.

This motoring guide promises a journey with stops at haunted hotels, covered bridges, lighthouses, waterfalls, mile-high mountains, Civil War sites, and seven state parks. The detailed directions and photos will lead travelers from sea level in the Tidewater region, through the Piedmont, to the Blue Ridge Highlands before they turn to the southwest.

The paths of many famous Americans are explored along this corridor, including those of Johnny Cash, Jefferson Davis, Douglas MacArthur, Gregory Peck, and George Washington. And many more odd and tempting stops beckon from listings such as "Confederate Graffiti," "The Real Mayberry," and "Fake Lake."

A bibliography and list of resources are included.

ISBN: 978-1-57072-323-0 • $17.95